Every Kid's Guide to
Good Manners

Written by
JOY BERRY

CHILDRENS PRESS ®
CHICAGO

About the Author and Publisher

Joy Berry's mission in life is to help families cope with everyday problems and to help children become competent, responsible, happy individuals. To achieve her goal, she has written over two hundred self-help books for children from birth through age twelve. Her work revolutionized children's publishing by providing families with practical, how-to, living skills information that was previously unavailable in children's books.

Joy gathered a dedicated team of experts, including psychologists, educators, child developmentalists, writers, editors, designers, and artists, to form her publishing company and to help produce her work.

The company, Living Skills Press, produces thoroughly researched books and audio-visual materials that successfully combine humor and education to teach subjects ranging from how to clean a bedroom to how to resolve problems and get along with other people.

Managing Editor: Ellen Klarberg
Copy Editor: Kate Dickey
Contributing Editors: Libby Byers, Maureen Dryden,
Yona Flemming, Gretchen Savidge
Editorial Assistant: Sandy Passarino

Art Director: Laurie Westdahl
Design: Abigail Johnston, Laurie Westdahl
Production: Abigail Johnston, Caroline Rennard
Illustrations designed by: Bartholomew
Inker: Berenice Happe Iriks
Colorer: Berenice Happe Iriks
Composition: Curt Chelin

Good manners can make life more pleasant for you and everyone around you.

EVERY KID'S GUIDE TO GOOD MANNERS will teach you how to have good manners when you

- meet other people for the first time,
- meet people who are disabled or have special needs,
- talk with other people,
- eat with other people,
- play with other people,
- work with other people,
- visit other people, and
- use other people's belongings.

You will also learn

- special words to say to other people and
- special things to do for other people.

When you have good manners, you treat other people the way you want to be treated.

When you treat other people the way you want to be
treated, you treat them with respect and kindness.
You are polite, considerate, and caring.

Try to be polite and courteous when you meet someone for the first time.

- Tell the person your name.
- Ask the person his or her name.
- Shake the person's hand if it is offered to you.
- Initiate a handshake by holding out your right hand.

- Be interested in the person.
- Encourage the person to talk.

Try to be respectful and kind when you meet someone who is disabled or has special needs.

- Avoid staring at the person for a long time.
- Avoid pointing at the person.
- Avoid whispering about the person.
- Avoid laughing or making fun of the person.

- Never do anything to hurt a disabled person, and never encourage anyone else to hurt the person.

It is understandable if you are curious about a person who is disabled. It is also understandable if you feel uncomfortable around him or her.

Learning about a person's disabilities might help you understand the disabled person better. Getting to know the person might help you overcome feeling uncomfortable around him or her.

Adults can provide you the information you need to have. Talk to an adult when the disabled person is not around.

You might discover that you can go directly to the disabled person and have more of your questions answered.

Try to be respectful and kind when you are talking with another person.

- Avoid doing *all* the talking.
- Avoid focusing the *entire* conversation on yourself and your interests.
- Avoid bragging.

- Be attentive when someone talks to you. Look at the person and listen to what is being said.
- Avoid interrupting someone who is talking. Allow the person to finish talking before you speak.
- Say "excuse me" if it becomes necessary to interrupt someone who is talking.

- Avoid saying things that might hurt other people.

- Talk softly if there are people around who might be bothered by loud talking.

Try to be polite and courteous when you eat with other people.

- Avoid eating in front of people who do not have food.

- Kindly ask the people who are sitting at the table to pass you things that are not close to you.
- Make sure everyone at the table has some food before you begin eating your meal.

- Avoid burping around other people.
- Say "excuse me" if you should accidentally burp.
- Cover your mouth, turn away from the food, and say "excuse me" if you must sneeze or cough while you are at the table.

- Avoid making a mess around you when you eat.
- Spread a napkin on your lap to catch food that you might accidentally drop.

- Avoid stuffing your mouth full of food.
- Avoid talking when you have food in your mouth.

- Ask permission to leave the table after you have finished eating.
- Offer to help clean up after everyone has finished eating the meal.
- Remember to thank the person who prepared the food.

Try to be respectful and kind when you play with other people.

- Share your belongings whenever possible.

• Let everyone who is involved take turns deciding what to play.

- Make sure that everyone who is going to play a game understands the rules and agrees to follow them.
- Avoid changing the rules while a game is being played unless every player wants to do so.

- Follow the rules of the game.
- Do not cheat.
- Be a good sport whether you win or lose.

Try to be polite and courteous when you work with other people.

- Do not put off working in the hope that you won't have to work at all. Begin working as soon as possible.

- Do not try to make another person do more work than you.
- Do your fair share of work.

• Avoid complaining while you work.

- Do your work well so that someone else will not have to do it again.
- Finish the work you start so that it will not have to be finished by another person.

Try to be respectful when you visit another person.

- Avoid misusing, damaging, or destroying anyone's property.

- Get the owner's permission before you go into a house or building.
- Avoid looking in another person's closets or drawers unless you have permission to do so.

- Wipe your feet before you enter a home or building so you will not track in mud, water, or dirt.

- Put things away when you finish using them.
- Put your trash in a trash can.
- Clean up any mess you make.

Try to be respectful when you use another person's belongings.

- Get the owner's permission before you use something that does not belong to you.

• Return anything you borrow as soon as possible.

- Avoid misusing or damaging another person's belongings.
- Avoid destroying or losing another person's belongings.

- Do your best to repair or replace any belonging you damage or lose. You might need an adult to help you do this.

Here are some special words that can help you show respect for other people:

- *How are you today?* Words to say when you greet someone or want to know how a person is.
- *Fine, thank you. How are you?* Words to say when a person asks you how you are. Try not to say these words unless you really do feel fine.
- *May I?* Words to say when you want permission to do something.
- *Please.* A word to say when you want something from someone else.
- *Thank you.* Words to say when you appreciate what someone has done for you or when another person has given you something.

- *No, thank you.* Words to say when a person offers you something you do not want.
- *You're welcome.* Words to say when a person thanks you for something.
- *Excuse me.* Words to say when you interrupt a person, bump into someone, interfere with what someone is doing, or hurt a person's feelings.
- *Pardon?* A word to say when you do not hear what someone says and you want the person to repeat it.
- *I'm sorry.* Words to say when you do something wrong to someone else.

Here are special things you can do to help another person:

- Help someone carry his or her load.
- Open a door for someone.
- Offer someone your seat if he or she needs it more than you do.
- When a person drops something, pick it up for him or her.

- Help a person when he or she is struggling to put on an article of clothing.
- Help a person who needs you to get something he or she needs.
- Do what you can to help a person who is upset.
- Do your best to help a person who gets hurt.

Here are some special things you can do to show respect for another person:

- Cover your mouth when you yawn, sneeze, or cough.

- Be as quiet as you can around people who are
  doing things such as
    sleeping,
    resting,
    talking,
    thinking,
    reading,
    watching a performance,
    listening to TV, a radio, or a record player.

- Try to be on time wherever you go.

- Take turns being first.
- Do not always insist on getting the biggest or the best for yourself.

• Step out of the way and let the other person pass when you meet a person walking directly toward you.

- Avoid walking between a person and the TV.
- Avoid walking between two people who are talking.

Good manners can make life more pleasant for you and everyone around you. When you have good manners, other people will appreciate you and enjoy being around you. They will also be more likely to treat you the way you want to be treated.

For this reason. . .